WITH GUNS AND DRUMS

Civil War Birmingham 1642 - 1645

Stephen L Wright

Second Edition

JACOBUS Publications

NEWTOWN

1997

With Guns and Drums

First published in 1997 by Jacobus Publications. JPB048.

Jacobus Publications
Clarinor Manor, Middle Scafell, Milford Road, Newtown, Powys,
SY16 3HQ.

British Library Cataloguing in Publication Data. A catalogue
record for this book is available from the British Library.

Designed and typeset by Bobby Bunny Press.
Printed and bound in Great Britain by Advanced Laser Press Ltd.

ISBN 1 898621 48 9

CONTENTS

Page 4   Preface

Page 5   Introduction

Page 6   "Soldier, soldier"

Page 10   Birmingham in 1642

Page 13   Battles and Sieges

Page 13   The Battle of Kings Norton   17 October 1642

Page 17   The Battle of Birmingham   4 April 1643

Page 21   The Siege of Aston Hall   26-27 December 1643

Page 24   The Siege of Hawkesley House   12-14 May 1645

Page 26   Three Thomases - Fox, Hall and Holte

Page 26   Col. "Thomas" Fox - The "Jovial Tinker"

Page 29   Rev. Thomas Hall - Curate and Schoolmaster at Kings Norton

Page 34   Sir Thomas Holte - First Master of Aston Hall

Page 38   Bibliography

ILLUSTRATIONS

Page 6   Pikeman at the Charge.

Page 7   Musketeer.

Page 9   A Dragoon and Cavalry Trooper.

Page 11   Musketeer Firing.

Page 12   Prince Rupert.

Page 15   The Green at Kings Norton.

Page 16   Woodcut of Prince Rupert.

Page 18   Aston Hall.

Page 20   The Long Gallery at Aston Hall.

Page 23   Scene from the Siege of Aston Hall.

Page 25   Woodcut of Civil War Soldiers.

Page 31   The House of Thomas Hall.

Page 33   The Schoolhouse in Kings Norton.

Page 34   Sir Thomas Holte.

Page 36   The Drawing Room At Aston Hall.

With Guns and Drums

Preface to the Second Edition

In 1989, when I first published "<u>With Guns and Drums</u>", I simply wanted to draw together some of the personalities and events from Birmingham's involvement in the first English Civil War which started in 1642.

Now, thanks to Peter Francis-Wemyss of Jacobus Publications, I have been given the opportunity to expand my 1989 manuscript and to give a much broader picture of Birmingham's involvement in the turbulent times of the first English Civil War.

I have retained the two main sections, Battles and Sieges and Three Thomases, from the first edition with additional sections on soldiers of the Civil Wars and Birmingham in 1642.

Stephen Wright
Birmingham 1997

Civil War Birmingham 1642 - 1645

Introduction

When Charles I raised his standard at Nottingham, on 22 August 1642, he formally declared the start of the first Civil War in England since the time of Richard III.

The English Civil Wars, as they are properly known, have been sadly misunderstood by several generations. The romantic portraits by Victorian artists have left us with the impression of a war fought between long-haired Cavaliers and crop-headed Puritans. Nothing could be further from the truth. It is true that the majority of the aristocracy supported the King, but several nobles fought on the side of Parliament. Contrary to popular belief, Oliver Cromwell was not the first leader of Parliament's forces. At the start of the first Civil War he had no military experience. It was Robert Deveraux, 3rd Earl of Essex, who was commissioned by Parliament to be Captain-General.

The Wars were *"...without an enemy..."*[1]. Families were divided according to their particular beliefs and loyalties. It is true that social and economic conditions, religion and politics all had a part to play in the spiral into armed conflict. However, the causes of the wars ran deeper than this. Since the previous century frictions between Crown and Parliament had been growing. Each wanted to have more control over all aspects of English life.

Attempts were made to resolve the differences. Eventually, though, no further bargaining achieved anything. The result was WAR.

---

1. "That great God who is the searcher of my heart knows with what a perfect hatred I detest this war *without an enemy....*" from a letter written by William Waller to his friend Ralph Hopton, shortly before they met in battle at Lansdown nr. Bath, July 1643.

'Soldier, soldier'

At the start of the Civil Wars there was no standing army. Each side had to recruit men by whatever means they could.

Armies were divided into two main branches - Foot and Horse. The former being further divided into pikemen and musketeers.

FOOT

The Pikeman

In the battles and sieges in and around Birmingham the gentlemen of the pike would have been a useful asset . Holding off the Horse at Kings Norton; driving the musketeers from the defences in Birmingham and Aston Hall; forming a wall of steel at Hawkesley House.

The pikeman was a fearsome spectacle. Heavily armoured with a backplate, breast plate and helmet, he carried an 18 foot ash pole topped with an iron spearhead.

Used efficiently, the pike was a formidable weapon. When held at the "Charge"

❖*A Pikeman at the Charge.*

❖ *A Musketeer making ready.*

(horizontal to the ground) or the "Port" (at an angle of 45°) by blocks of pikemen it would make these blocks v i r t u a l l y unbreakable.

Pikemen were used to protect the musketeers and to drive wedges through the opposing pike blocks.

The Musketeer

The musketeer wore no armour. His weapon, the matchlock musket, was usually around 4" feet in length. This made it very unwieldy. A rest was used to assist in steadying the musket when firing.

Powder for the main charge was carried in wooden or leather tubes. These hung from a bandolier. Priming powder was carried in a flask. Musket balls and wadding, which kept the ball from rolling out of the barrel, were kept in a pouch.

The matchlock musket got its name from the slowmatch which was used to ignite the powder. Match was made by boiling cord in a saltpetre solution. A length of match, often with both ends lit, was carried in the hand. Spare lengths were fastened round the waist or hat.

When ready to fire his musket, the musketeer would fasten one end of the match in the jaws of the lock. A crude trigger would pull the lock down and the match would, hopefully, ignite the priming charge. Misfires were not uncommon!

Muskets were accurate to about 80 yards, but with blocks of men as the target it was almost impossible to miss.

HORSE

The Cavalry Trooper

In the opening stages of the Wars the cavalry trooper was someone already able to ride. It was not till much later that men were trained as cavalry.

The trooper was generally protected by armour similar to the pikeman, with the exception of tassets. He carried a sword and a pair of pistols.

Cavalry flanked the Foot. They were used as skirmishing troops to harry and break the opposition.

In addition to the Foot and Horse were:

THE DRAGOON

Falling between the Foot and Horse, the dragoon was, in essence, a mounted foot soldier. He rode to his fighting position and then dismounted to continue fighting on foot.

The dragoon's main weapon was the carbine. Somewhat

shorter than the matchlock musket, it could be attached by a swivel to a shoulder strap whilst riding.

Dragoons were good troops to use from ambush and it is fairly certain that, at Hawkesley House, Astley would have used them to great effect in setting up a firing position from which they could cover the advance of the rest of their fellows.

ARTILLERY

Cannon were seldom used in the set battle situation. Those that were were usually small field pieces which could be moved quickly around the fighting. It is most likely that it was this kind of artillery piece which was the main protagonist at Aston Hall.

❖*A Dragoon.*   ❖*A Cavalry Trooper.*

Birmingham in 1642

Birmingham, at the heart of the country, had been an important trading centre for several centuries. However, it must not be assumed that because of its importance Birmingham was a large and imposing town. It was simply a prospering provincial centre.

Nevertheless, by 1642, the metal-working industry which had evolved in and around the town had led to it being a highly acclaimed leader in the field of sword-making. This was an extension of Birmingham's place as a major centre of the cutlery trade.

Perhaps the best way to "visit" the Birmingham of 1642 is through the eyes of a merchant on business. He approaches the town from the south-east and passes the Old Ship Inn, which has come down to our time as the traditional headquarters of Prince Rupert at the Battle of Birmingham, and a glance to his left gives him an excellent prospect of Stratford House, built by Ambrose Rotton about 1601. Leaving these two dwellings behind him, the merchant passes few others until he sees the Old Crown Inn ahead. He may well have read John Leland's account of his visit to Birmingham and formed a mental picture of this *"mansion house of tymber"*. He rides up to the inn and decides to make this his base for his time in the town. Having taken a tankard of ale with his Host, our merchant has a desire to walk up the hill into the High Town area.

He enters Deritend passing St John's Chapel, daughter chapel of Aston Parish, on his left, crosses the Rea and reaches Digbeth. Here his ears are assailed by a veritable army of smiths turning out their blades. Continuing up the hill he soon reaches St Martin's Church showing its age but still the only church for the townsfolk of Birmingham.

Passing the east end of St Martin's, our merchant walks through the Shambles past the Market Cross and into the High Town. Here is the Free School and the Leather Hall on the road to Stourbridge. He walks along the Beast Market and comes to

❖*A Musketeer firing.*

the road to Wolverhampton and Walsall, along which rival troopers will chase each other during the Battle of Birmingham. A plain stone pillar, with a short cross-piece, on a rough-hewn pedestal stands at the junction of the two roads. This is the Welch Cross, later to be replaced by a much grander structure.

Retracing his steps to the Market Cross, the merchant passes St Martin's at its western end and comes to Mercer Street. Here are the mercers' shops, where our merchant hopes to do business. He will not stop now, but carries on his tour by turning right into Edgbaston Street and takes a few moments to view the moated rectory of St Martin's. Retracing his steps once more he walks past the south side of St Martin's and into Moat Lane where the moated manor house of Birmingham stands. Passing the house he turns left into Upper Mill Lane and at its end is once more in Digbeth.

A walk down the hill brings our merchant back to the Old Crown where a welcome jug of claret and a meal await him.

❖*Prince Rupert.*

BATTLE AND SIEGES

The Midlands is often referred to as the "Cockpit of England" since so much fighting has taken place in this region. The following accounts of the fighting which took place in and around Birmingham are typical of the majority of engagements which made up the Civil Wars. Very few major set-piece battles took place.

* * * * * * *

The Battle of Kings Norton

Kings Norton, according to Domesday, was a berewick of Bromsgrove. It belonged to the Crown, hence the royal name. For many years the village was known as Norton-juxta-Bromsgrove.

The village was a peaceful place inhabited by wool staplers and yeoman farmers. On his marriage to Henrietta Maria, Charles I had given her the Manor of Kings Norton as part of his dowry. In 1639, the Queen attempted to "improve" her lands by having the best pasture enclosed. This was fiercely contested by her tenants and may very well have been a major reason for the village taking the side of Parliament when war was declared.

In October 1642, Prince Rupert, nephew of Charles I, was moving to meet his uncle to join forces on what was to be the eve of the first major conflict of the war. The route of the march took the Prince and his men from Stourbridge eastwards through Hagley and over Clent. The following is a facsimile of the preamble of a Parliamentarian tract:

13

A TRUE
RELATION
OF A
G R E A T   A N D   C R U E L L

Battell fought by the Lord Willoughby of Parham with 800. Horse and Foot who were going to the L. Generall, against Prince Robert with 9 Troops of Horse, and 300. Foot neer Brumegum in Warwicke-shire, October the 17.

Declaring also the manner of the L. Wiloughbies obtaining the Victory, killing about 50 of the Cavaleers, and taking 20 prisoners, with the loss of 20 men.

Sent in Letter from His Excellencie to the House of Commons, and read in the said House, October 18
Printed for Richard West October 20

Only this one account of the encounter exists and that only in memory since the original, part of a valuable collection of Warwickshire books, prints and manuscripts was destroyed in the fire which consumed Birmingham Library in 1879.

Other Birmingham writers place the battle in Moseley and the name of Captain Greaves (see The Battle of Birmingham) is sometimes mentioned. If ever a battle did take place it would have been, like so many other "battles" of the Civil Wars, nothing more than a skirmish. It is extremely unlikely that

❖ *The Green at Kings Norton.*

such an experienced soldier as Prince Rupert would have been routed by someone like Willoughby of Parham. The thing is, we will never know. Just another mystery lost in the mists of time.

The village of Kings Norton, although a suburb of Birmingham, retains its character with its church, pub and bailiff's house grouped around the green. It is well worth a visit and lies on the A441 between Alvechurch and Selly Oak.

❖ *A Contemporary Woodcut of Prince Rupert, with Birmingham in the background.*

16

Civil War Birmingham 1642 - 1645

The Battle Of Birmingham

I know of two stories which purport to explain the reason for Prince Rupert's attack on Birmingham. The first is about its citizens who attacked and plundered the supply train belonging to the King which was being taken to help in the relief of Banbury Castle. The second, according to a *'Letter from Walshall'*, says the town's mills supplied 15,000 swords to the Earl of Essex's forces and *"not only refused to supply the King's forces with swords for their money, but imprisoned diverse who bought swords, upon suspicion that they intended to supply the King's forces with them."*

Unlike Kings Norton, there is no doubt that a battle did take place in Birmingham on 4 April 1643. Accounts, like the *'Letter from Walshall'*, abound and are documented in many Birmingham histories. Most significant in all these accounts is the reference to Rupert's burning of the town. Numbers of houses which were burnt down vary from account to account. The above mentioned letter speaks of the *"...miserable destruction of Burmingham by fire..."*. Most accounts say that between 80 and 100 houses were destroyed. Why did his Highness feel the need to fire the town? To understand this we must look at the events of that fateful Easter Monday.

About 3:00 in the afternoon, the Prince's army was seen approaching the town. The people of Birmingham were prepared for such an encounter and had raised barricades across the main roads into the town. The Prince's route of march brought him down from Camp Hill into Deritend. Facing him across the barricades were 140 musketeers and a company of Troopers led by Captain Greaves. The Prince asked for passage into the town and was, much to his consternation, both verbally and by musket volley refused. The men of Birmingham were

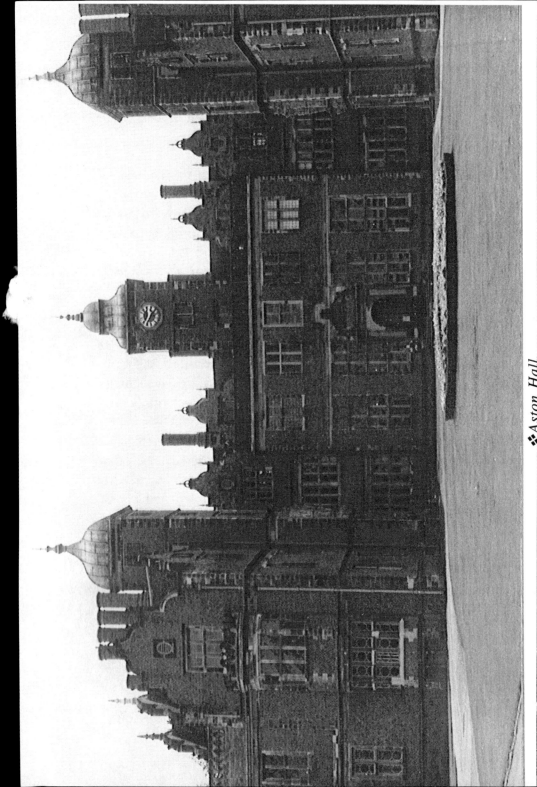

❖ *Aston Hall*

said to have called the Prince and his soldiers "*Cursed doggs, develish Cavaliers* (and) *Popish Traytors*". They twice fended off two attacks made on their defensive works.

Finding no direct way into the town, the Prince was forced to lead his army across the marshy fields of the Rea Valley. As they entered the town from this direction, the Royalists were met with musket fire from the houses. The author of the wonderfully entitled pamphlet "*Prince Rupert's Burning Love To England As Discovered In Birmingham's Flames*" recalls that the King's soldiers replied to this assault by shooting "*..at every door or window where they could espy any looking out* (and) *they hacked, hewed or pistolled all they met with, without distinction, blaspheming* (and) *cursing most hideously*".

Captain Greaves and his men were pursued through the town by a company commanded by Basil Feilding, 1st Earl of Denbigh. The pursuit ended at Shireland Road, Bearwood when Greaves rallied his men and fired a shot at the enemy. Denbigh fell, mortally wounded and the Parliamentarian Troopers fled to Lichfield.

Back in the town, the Royalists finally took control. According to all eye-witnesses it was under the orders of the Prince that the burning began. In his "History of Birmingham", Hutton reports that Rupert's "*wrath is said to have kindled in Bull Street and consumed several houses near the spot, now No. 12*". Yet, even then, there is still some doubt as to whether the Prince did authorise this destruction. But there is no doubt that this act, whether by his orders or not, still led to Rupert being hated by the townspeople of Birmingham.

Today, Deritend and other streets where fighting took place would not really be recognised by any of the battle's

participants. Mills and blade shops have given way to factory units, car showrooms and the city's main coach station. One building, however, has stood the test of time. The Old Crown Inn, whose future at the time of writing is under consideration, stands on the corner of Deritend and Heath Mill Lane. Built in the 14 Century, the inn would have played some part in the in the events of the battle. Sadly, at present, it is closed and therefore does not allow one to sit by its once roaring fire and soak up something of the atmosphere of Easter Monday, 1643.

The Siege of Aston Hall

The events in Birmingham left a sour taste in the mouths of its inhabitants. Rupert might have gone but the feeling of vengeance was still very strong. Anyone showing the least interest in supporting the King would, in the eyes of Birmingham citizens, be a legitimate target for an unleashing of that vengeance.

On the outskirts of the town, at Aston Hall, Sir Thomas Holte was not a happy man. He had owned several of the houses burned by Rupert's troops. He was also afraid for himself and his family. It was common knowledge that the Holtes were Royalists. Sir Thomas needed help.

In December, 1643, he wrote to Colonel Leveson at Dudley Castle and asked him to supply some men to set up a small, but defiant, garrison at the Hall. Forty musketeers duly arrived on the 18th. Their officer wanted to fell trees, which could act as cover for an attacking force, and construct earthworks. Sir Thomas was not so sure but, reluctantly, allowed his grounds to be dug up. The parish church which lies outside Aston Hall's wall was used as a stronghold. The garrison was ready.

❖ *The Long Gallery at Aston Hall.*

In the town the preparations did not go unnoticed. The Warwickshire Committee, Parliament's local governing body, was alerted and Colonel Bosville, at the Coventry garrison, was ordered to *"...reduce the house"*. He arrived on Boxing Day at the head of a force of 1200 men and challenged the defenders to surrender. They refused so Bosville bombarded the Hall with cannon-fire.

The following day the Parliamentarian troops made a valiant frontal assault on the Royalist positions taking both church and defenders. From this stronghold they were able to make a further assault on the Hall. The earthworks were over-run and entry was gained to the Hall. Its defenders called for quarter (an honourable request which meant surrender with no further loss of life). Bosville granted them quarter but, for what reason we will never know, they continued to fight. This was an outrageous move and could quite easily have cost them their lives. Peace was reached and Sir Thomas and his men were taken prisoner and *"sent to Coventry"*.

Now it may seem no strange thing that a force of 40 should be overwhelmed by one some thirty times larger. But all is not as it first appears. There is no way that Colonel Bosville could have brought such a strong unit from Coventry. It seems much more likely that his men were supplemented by men from Birmingham. These latter, despite the brave defence of their town some eight months earlier, were not seasoned soldiers and were therefore motivated more by spirit than discipline.

The Hall suffered some considerable damage. A newel post on the main staircase was shattered and can still be seen in this state. A small glass case holds some cannon balls found inside the Hall after the siege.

❖*A scene from the Siege of Aston Hall. A cannonball has just struck the newel post of the main staircase.*

With Guns and Drums

The Siege of Hawkesley House

Nothing now remains of Hawkesley House, and even its site is disputed, but it must have been an impressive place. It was owned by the Middlemores, a prominent Catholic family.

In early 1645, Col Fox, of whom more later, evicted the Middlemores and moved into Hawkesley. He was not a stranger to Middlemore property having garrisoned their house at Edgbaston in the previous year. A Capt Gough was placed in command of the Hawkesley garrison.

On 11 May, the headquarters of the Royalist army was at Bromsgrove. The Journal of Richard Symonds, an officer with Prince Rupert, gives us an eyewitness account of the taking of Hawkesley House:

> "His Majesty, with his own regiment of foot and horsegaurds only, marched from Inkborough magna to Saltwiche, where he stayed till Wednesday. In the meantime Prince Rupert set down before Hawkesley House, belonging to one Mr Middlemore. Lord Astley's tertia of foot made the approaches which were left for us, with great advantage, viz. , banks, a lake and trees. Captain Backster of the Horse was killed here, and some foot soldiers and pioneers. On Wednesday about two o'clock in the afternoon, the King left Wiche, and went with his guards to the leaguer before Hawkesley; and just as His Majesty appeared in view, it was delivered unto the mercy of the King and his officers, on condition that they might be free from the insolence of common soldiers. In the house were found a month's provisions and

ammunition; but the soldiers would not fight, when they perceived it was the King's army. The son of Dr Gouge was the captain, andgovernor, and Whichcot commanded the horse. There were 60 foot, and above 40 horse. After Lord Astley had pillaged the house, and taken the soldiers prisoners, the house was set on fire".

That there was so much powder and shot and a month's supply of provisions can only lead to the conclusion that, but for the arrival of the King, the house's defenders would have fought on. The razing of the house was common policy to prevent its use by Fox or any other malignants. Presumably the Middlemores were compensated.

❖*Contemporary woodcut of Civil War Soldiers on the March.*

Sotheby's © 1994.

Three Thomases - Fox, Hall and Holte

It just so happens that three men who had a notable effect on Birmingham and its surrounding area at the time of the Civil Wars were all called Thomas - or so the local history books would have us believe with Col Fox. As with any historical figure, documented evidence of their life is a valuable asset and there is plenty available on Hall and Holte. Fox is something of an enigma, as you will read below. Nevertheless, collectively, the three men are good examples of the Soldier, the Churchman and the Gentry. Their lives mirror the experience of many others from their particular place in 17 Century society, especially during the time of the Civil Wars.

* * * * * * *

Colonel 'Thomas' Fox - The 'Jovial Tinker'

Every book on Birmingham and the Civil War, which includes any reference to Fox, gives his first name as Thomas - a case of writer copying writer and not researching? His real name was John and there are a number of references to him in "The Calendar of State Papers" - (1641-44) Vol 18. Since finding these references, I am now able to include some further gems about his work in the cause of Parliament.

Fox first came to the notice of the people of England through the columns of "*Mercurius Aulicus*", the Royalist news-sheet, in February, 1644. In the previous year he had raised a troop of Horse and been appointed its Colonel by the Worcester Committee. These troopers, some of whom we met at

Hawkesley House, were chosen on their colonel's understanding of what made a *"good"* soldier. On the whole, they were loyal and responded to Fox's enthusiasm.

As with many characters who arise out of all civil wars, Fox's origins are shrouded in myth and legend. Variously, he hails from Birmingham, Dudley, Tamworth and Walsall. As to his character, most sources agree that Fox was a typical specimen of the fighting Puritan. In other words, he was a man who was either in a *"...passion or a prayer"*.

From whichever town Fox came, he used the Midlands, especially the area around Birmingham, as the centre for his work. We know of at least three houses which he garrisoned for Parliament. That at Hawkesley has already been mentioned in some detail. The manors at Edgbaston, owned by Richard Middlemore, and Stourton Castle, former home of Cardinal Reginald Pole, also fell to Fox's men.

Edgbaston was taken in 1644. Parliament acknowledged the way in which Fox had *"...possessed himself of* (the house) *with great courage* (and had) *fortified and garrisoned it with 400 horse and foot"* In recognition of his action, Fox was *"...empowered to hold and enjoy the mansion house and manor of Edgbaston, together with the rents and revenues payable to Richard Middlemore in the parishes of Kings Norton, Yardley and Northfield in co. Worcester"*.

Unlike Hawkesley, records do not seem to exist as to Edgbaston's recapture, but recaptured it was. There is, however, a letter from Fox to the Earl of Denbigh, whose father was killed at the Battle of Birmingham, military head of Parliament's Midland Association. Fox complains about the delay of provisions to the garrison and warns his Lordship that the garrison *"..needs no enemy to destroy it, for if money be not supplied, it will destroy itself"*. It would appear that destruction was indeed on the minds of the men at Edgbaston for there was considerable damage done to the parish church. Lead was stripped from the roof for musket shot, and stones from the churchyard wall were used for strengthening the defences around the house. Parliament was so concerned about the situation at Edgbaston that it called a meeting for representatives from the Worcester, Warwick and Stafford committees to talk with Fox about contributions towards the garrison. Following this meeting, Parliament ordered the Worcester Committee to pay Fox £70 per week for the upkeep of a troop of Horse. For some reason, known only to Parliament, this order was recinded in the September.

From Edgbaston, Fox led a raid on the walled town of Bewdley which was governed by Sir Thomas Lyttleton of Frankley, near Birmingham. However, with a hand-picked troop of sixty men, Fox rode to Bewdley and overcame it by stealth. The sleepy guards at the bridge fell, literally, for Fox's story of his men being part of Prince Rupert's force. As the troopers passed by, the two guards were unceremoniously despatched into the river. On entering the town, Fox and his men made for Sir Thomas Lyttleton's residence at the top end of Bewdley. All was surprise at this place and the governor was persuaded to surrender his charge. Along with Sir Thomas, who was eventually taken to London, Fox and his men also took away several Flanders mares.

Yet even Bewdley was not enough for the Tinker. He had his eye set on another gem - Stourton Castle. This fine home stood on a rise overlooking the valley of the River Stour. Down close to the river was a series of smithies which produced arms for the local area. Fox was determined to take control of this supply and led a party of 300 men to attempt a capture. The castle fell and Fox set up another garrison.

As with much of the rest of Fox's life, an apocryphal tale has come to us about his time at Stourton. It is said that the Tinker was leading a patrol across the heath close to the castle when Prince Rupert and a patrol came into view. Fox ordered his men to charge the enemy and the latter turned and fled. Coming to the Oldswinford Gate, the Prince saw it was closed but a boy stood nearby. His Highness shouted to the boy to open the gate, and the startled young fellow obeyed. He had the foresight to close the gate after the Prince's men and for his loyalty was given a ring which he was told to present at Court when the King returned. Did he go to London? Did such an event ever happen?

There is another question which defies answer. No-one knows what happened to Fox. Perhaps he returned to his trade. Perhaps he was killed. However, so great was the Royalists loathing for him that they named him as the executioner of Charles I. The Tinker's ultimate exploit? Who knows?

Rev Thomas Hall, BD - Curate and Schoolmaster at Kings Norton

Thomas Hall was born in Worcester in July, 1610. His father, Richard, was a wealthy clothier and sent his son to be educated at the King's School. It was a well made decision. The keen spirit and quick mind of Thomas was soon picked up by his tutor, Henry Bright, who suggested to Richard Hall that he enter the boy at Balliol College, Oxford. This took place, but Thomas only remained one term at Balliol before moving to Pembroke College. His new tutor was Thomas Lushington, later to become chaplain to Charles I. The Thomas's did not see eye to eye. The ideas of the younger, particularly with regard to theology and politics, began to flourish. He disagreed so much with his tutor's views on theology that he published a condemnatory treatise - his first of many.

Hall completed his degree in 1628, took up a teaching post at Warwick Grammar School and, after his ordination, became curate and schoolmaster at Kings Norton. Described as a *"...plain and fervent preacher"*, Hall no doubt laid many of his opinions on parishioners and pupils alike. He developed his interest in writing and had several books published. He began a library in the school which received several of his books.

The effect of the War on Kings Norton has already been spoken of, but Hall also suffered for his beliefs. He was a staunch anti-Royalist and not afraid of saying so. When Henrietta Maria and her army arrived in Kings Norton in July, 1643, Hall's heart must have sunk. There is little doubt that he would have been "inconvenienced" by the soldiers. Indeed, apocryphal tale has it that Hall's home was ransacked and he was made the butt of the soldiers' fun. There is perhaps more in the account that lead was stripped from the church for making shot. Whatever, 3000 Horse, 30 companies of Foot, several artillery pieces and a baggage train would have made quite a mess of the village.

Parliament's victory in 1651 must have brought nothing less than unparalleled joy to Hall. In the 1650's he joined the Presbyterian Classis based at Kenilworth and became a regular "lecturer" at St Martin's in Birmingham. Hall's pamphlet writing increased, mainly against the radical sectaries.

❖ *The House of Thomas Hall.*

With Guns and Drums

One of his most famous pamphlets was written in 1651 and is entitled *"The Pulpit Guarded with XX Arguments"*. In this, Hall seeks to prove the *"...Unlawfulness, Sinfulness and Danger of suffering Private persons to take upon them Publike* (sic) *Preaching and expounding the Scriptures without a Call..."*. This is *"...contrary to the Word of God* (and) *to the practice of all Reformed Churches..."*. Therefore, *"...let the nailer keep to his hammer, the husbandman his plough, the tailor to his shears, the baker to his kneading trough, the miller to his toll, the tanner to his hides and the sodier to his arms etc...let them keep the bounds and limits of their particular callings...Ministers must study and preach, people must hear and obey."*

From 1650-1662, Hall published twenty volumes of his works. In 1652 he received a B.D. from Oxford - the Vice-Chancellor at the time was a certain Oliver Cromwell!

The 1662 Act of Uniformity led to Thomas Hall's ejection from Kings Norton. The Act, designed to reintroduce all practices contained in the Book of Common Prayer, was opposed by 2000 Church of England clergy. On 17 August churches were packed as people flocked to hear final sermons before the Oath of Assent was to be taken. The folk of Kings Norton must have been very despondent. For thirty years Thomas Hall had acted as spiritual guide and friend - even though he had condemned May Poles and Fairs! He left in poverty, adamant in his Presbyterianism.

The life of Thomas Hall had been *"...an holy and unblameless..."* one. Now his health suffered badly, but he was not forgotten in his illness. Down to his last sixpence, his faith remained strong and was rewarded by his receiving *"...several packets of money..."*. he died on 13 April 1665 and was buried in the churchyard of the place he had served so faithfully.

❖ *The Schoolhouse in Kings Norton.*

Thomas Holte - First Master of Aston Hall

The Holte family has a history stretching back to the 14 Century when Simon del Holte acquired the manor of Nechells. This owning of property continued until the Holtes were a powerful landed family.

Thomas Holte was born in 1571. His father, Edward, wanted the best for his son. So, in 1588, Thomas went up to Magdalen College, Oxford, where the family enjoyed privilege of status. Two years later he entered the Inns of Court where he received the minimum legal training required by all prospective landowners of his standing.

❖Sir Thomas Holt.

In 1603 he was created Sir Thomas by James I. Eight years later he was made a baronet. Sir Thomas Holte, Bart. was now an extremely powerful man, especially in politics. He served as Deputy Lieutenant of Warwickshire, taking orders directly from the Privy Council in London.

Although he had a house in Duddeston, Sir Thomas wanted to build a house in the new style which was so popular throughout the country. In April, 1618, work began on Aston Hall. Its site had been chosen for reasons which would make it visible from all sides. By May, 1631, building was advanced enough for the family to move in. Four years later, the Hall was complete.

Warwickshire was deeply divided over loyalties to King and Parliament. In 1642, when war was declared, Sir Thomas took the side of Charles I. On the evening of 18 October, five days before Edgehill, the king slept at Aston Hall.

The siege of Christmas, 1643, has already been described. Following his arrest, after the storming of the Hall, Sir Thomas was taken to Coventry and his estates were sequestered. He was released after a short while.

Sir Thomas' troubles were not over. His land remained under the control of Parliament and in 1648 he was sequestered again for the events of 1643. Complaining bitterly about being charged twice with the same offence, Sir Thomas managed to keep the case going for over a year. It was all in vain and he was charged with being a "*delinquent*". His fine was set at '4,491 2s. 4d.' and was paid by February, 1652.

You may have some sympathy for Thomas Holte and his suffering. However, locally, he is remembered as the bad baron who killed his cook. The alleged crime took place in 1606 at

Duddeston Manor. The head cook at Duddeston was renowned for his culinary skills and his punctuality for serving food was something his master often boasted about.

On the fateful day in question, Sir Thomas was out hunting with his lawyer Richard Smallbrooke and other friends. In an effort to cheer his friend, Smallbrooke wagered his own best horse against the punctuality of the Duddeston head cook. The challenge was accepted, Sir Thomas never doubting the reliability of his man.

The party returned to the house to find the cook unprepared. Outraged by this, and the taunts of his friends, Sir Thomas is said to have taken a meat cleaver and split the cook's head in two. A neighbour, William Ascrick, claimed that:

> *"Sir Thomas tooke a cleaver and hit his cook with the same cleaver uppon the heade, and clave his heade, that on one syde thereof fell uppone one of his shoulders, and the other syde on the other   shoulder: and this I will veryfie to be trewe."*

The case eventually reached the Court of the King's Bench. Damages were reduced, although judgement was found in Ascrick's favour, since the defendant did not testify that the blow was fatal! Sir Thomas did not deny the charge and there would seem to be a strong probability that he did commit the murder as stated.

Thomas Holte died in 1654 at the grand old age of eighty-four. Despite the above slur, he should really be remembered as the man who left us one of the finest Jacobean houses in Britain. Judge for yourself. The Hall is open during the afternoon from 2-5 pm.

❖*The Drawing Room at Aston Hall.*

Bibliography

The Civil War in the Midlands - R E Sherwood (1992)

The Diary of the Marches of the Royal Army by Richard Symonds - C E Long (ed)   (1895)

The English Civil War, 1642-1651, An Illustrated History - Philip Haythornthwaite(1983)

The English Civil War, A Living History - Paul Lewis Isemonger (1995)

Brassey's History of Uniforms, English Civil War - Philipp J.C. Elliot-Wright   (1997)

The English Civil War - Maurice Ashley (1990)

Rupert of the Rhine - Maurice Ashley (1976)

Picture Credits

Pages 6, 7, 11, 12, 20, 23, 36; Peter Francis-Wemyss. Pages 15, 18, 31, 32; The Author. Page 25; Courtesy of Sotheby's. Page 16; Private Collection. Pages 9, 34; David Appleby.

ALSO AVAILABLE FROM

JACOBUS Publications

CROMWELL'S SOLDIERS: THE MOULDING OF THE NEW MODEL ARMY 1644- 1645

Barry Denton FRHistS   ISBN 1 898621 91 8   £9.95

This is without a doubt one of the most important works on the New Model Army to be published in recent years. Mr. Denton, a Fellow of the Royal Historical Society, is now widely recognised as one of the foremost authorities on the English Civil War, and particularly the NMA.

A LOYAL SUBJECT: THE LIFE OF SIR VINCENT CORBET AND HIS SHROPSHIRE DRAGOONS

By Peter Francis-Wemyss & Stephen Pickstock

ISBN 1 898621 18 7   £6.50

This is the most comprehensive study of this Royalist dragoon commander. Many years of research have gone into this work, making it the most detailed and accurate analysis of the Civil War in Shropshire and the part played by Corbet, who commanded his regiment until the end of the first Civil War in 1646.

MISTRESS JANE LANE

By C. Penruddocke   ISBN 1 898621 47 0   51pp   £4.50

A great many contemporary documents are used to tell the story of Jane Lane, who helped Charles II escape to France, after the Battle of Worcester.

A LARGE DECLARATION OF THE LATE TUMULTS IN SCOTLAND.

By Charles I.   430pp   ISBN 1 898621 60 8   £16.95
Due Early 1998.

A facsimile reprint of the first edition of this very important tract. This strongly worded work on the Bishop's Wars and build up to the Civil War, was written by King Charles I with the assistance of his chaplain, Walter Balcanquhall.

THE BOSCOBEL TRACT

ISBN 1 898621   46pp   £3

This is a reprint of the detailed and exciting pamphlet, of the exciting escape of Charles II, after the Battle of Worcester. Originally published in 1660, the writer based this account on the testimony's of those who helped the King escape. An important work.

IN WHOSE NAME: The Book of Seventeenth Century Christian Names

Peter Francis-Wemyss ISBN 1 898621 09 8   46pp   £3.50

The most complete dictionary of names in use during the mid seventeenth century. This work shows which were the most popular, along with a study of regional variations and the unusual. Well illustrated.

CHILDHOOD IN STUART BRITAIN

David Appleby   ISBN 1 898621 41 1   £2.95

The experiences of growing up in the first half of the seventeenth century and the Civil War period. An excellent read for adults, as well as being aimed at children.

CLUN AND ITS NEIGHBOURHOOD IN THE CIVIL WAR
The Rev. A. M. Auden   ISBN 1 898621 35 7   51pp   £4.95
An in-depth study of how the Civil War effected Clun, and its neighbouring towns in Shropshire and Montgomeryshire, with a detailed account of the part played by Clun Castle.

FIRE AND SWORD ALONG THE MARCHES
Edited By John Lewis   ISBN 1 898621 14 4   £6.50
An outstanding and finely detailed study of the Civil War in the Marcher Counties along the Welsh border. This work contains an immense amount of information. Very well illustrated.

MAY IT PLEASE YOUR HIGHNESS
Edited By John Lewis   ISBN 1 898621 32 2   £7.50
Limited Edition Hardback of 50 Copies   £17.50
This very important collection of letters to Prince Rupert, have never before been printed in their entirety. Historian John Lewis, has spent several years researching and annotating these letters. The writers of these exciting letters include: the Earl of Northampton, Arthur Lord Capel, the Earl of Crawford, Sir William Russell, Sir William Vavasour, General Charles Gerard, Captain Thomas Sandford, Sir John Mennes, Sir Michael Woodhouse, and Prince Maurice. This major work contains a wealth of information, and is illustrated.

MY FIRELOCKS USE NOT TO PARLEY
By Peter Francis-Wemyss   ISBN 1 898621 01 2   £3.50
My Firelocks reveals Hawarden Castle's important role in the English Civil War. This comprehensive study also reprints many original letters, and is very well illustrated.

PARLIAMENTS MAJOR GENERAL: THE CORRESPONDENCE AND PAPERS OF GENERAL THOMAS MYTTON

Edited by Peter Francis-Wemyss   ISBN 1 898621 87 X
£6.50   Due Early 1998.

This book contains a plethora of both military and private correspondence from and to this Parliamentarian officer, who held command in Shropshire, and then as General of North Wales. The letters are complimented by an in-depth biography of General Mytton.

OUR FALL OUR FAME:
THE LIFE AND TIMES OF SIR CHARLES LUCAS

By David Appleby   ISBN 1 898621 45 4   £11.95

An excellent study of one of the Civil War's best cavalry commanders, which is also the first major biography of this Royalist commander. Lucas was executed after the Siege of Colchester, and here the author has finally revealed the truth to show whether he was a martyr or villain? Well Illustrated.

VALOUR IS THE SAFEST HELM

By Paul Leask BA   ISBN 1 898621 10 1   SS   52p   £4.50

This book on Sir Hugh Cholmley, and the siege of Scarborough is meticulously researched. The study covers Cholmley's military activities from the Bishops Wars through to the end of the first Civil War. Very well illustrated.

YOUR MOST HUMBLE AND MOST OBLIGED SERVANT

Edited By John Lewis   ISBN 1 898621 13 6   26p   £3.95

A set of ten important letters by Lord John Byron, relating to the English Civil War in the Border Marches. The major topics of the letters concern activities around the Garrisons of Chester and Shrewsbury, and the Battle of Montgomery.